The Antarctic Habitat

Introducing Habitats

Molly Aloian and Bobbie Kalman

🌳 Crabtree Publishing Company

www.crabtreebooks.com

Created by Bobbie Kalman

Dedicated by Candice Murphy
To my daughter Emily, whose inner strength and confidence show her wonderful personality!
I am so very proud of you! My love always, Mom.

Editor-in-Chief
Bobbie Kalman

Writing team
Molly Aloian
Bobbie Kalman

Substantive editor
Kathryn Smithyman

Editors
Michael Hodge
Kelley MacAulay
Rebecca Sjonger

Design
Katherine Kantor
Samantha Crabtree
    (cover and series logo)

Production coordinator
Heather Fitzpatrick

Photo research
Crystal Foxton

Special thanks to
Jack Pickett and Karen Van Atte

Illustrations
Barbara Bedell: pages 15, 17 (magnifying glass & plankton), 18 (top), 19 (bottom),
    24, 26, 32 (orca & krill)
Katherine Kantor: page 32 (seal & grass)
Bonna Rouse: pages 17 (background), 18 (bottom), 19 (top), 20,
    21 (all except clams), 32 (cod)
Margaret Amy Salter: page 21 (clams)

Photographs
SeaPics.com: © Franco Banfi: page 25; © Phillip Colla: page 28;
    © Michael S. Nolan: pages 30-31
Visuals Unlimited: Gerald & Buff Corsi: pages 14, 16; Fritz Polking: page 12
Other images by Corel, Digital Stock, Digital Vision, and Eyewire

Library and Archives Canada Cataloguing in Publication

Aloian, Molly
    The Antarctic habitat / Molly Aloian & Bobbie Kalman.
(Introducing habitats)
Includes index.
ISBN-13: 978-0-7787-2956-3 (bound)
ISBN-10: 0-7787-2956-7 (bound)
ISBN-13: 978-0-7787-2984-6 (pbk.)
ISBN-10: 0-7787-2984-2 (pbk.)
    1. Ecology--Antarctica--Juvenile literature. I. Kalman,
Bobbie, date. II. Title. III. Series.

QH84.2.A46 2006   j577.0911'6   C2006-904089-3

Library of Congress Cataloging-in-Publication Data

Aloian, Molly.
    The Antarctic habitat / Molly Aloian & Bobbie Kalman.
    p. cm. -- (Introducing habitats)
Includes index.
ISBN-13: 978-0-7787-2956-3 (rlb)
ISBN-10: 0-7787-2956-7 (rlb)
ISBN-13: 978-0-7787-2984-6 (pb)
ISBN-10: 0-7787-2984-2 (pb)
    1. Ecology--Antarctica--Juvenile literature.   I. Kalman, Bobbie.
II. Title.
QH84.2.A46 2007
577.0911'6--dc22

2006018060

Crabtree Publishing Company

www.crabtreebooks.com   1-800-387-7650

Published in Canada
Crabtree Publishing
616 Welland Ave.
St. Catharines, ON
L2M 5V6

Published in the United States
Crabtree Publishing
PMB16A
350 Fifth Ave., Suite 3308
New York, NY 10118

Published in the United Kingdom
Crabtree Publishing
White Cross Mills
High Town, Lancaster
LA1 4XS

Published in Australia
Crabtree Publishing
386 Mt. Alexander Rd.
Ascot Vale (Melbourne)
VIC 3032

Contents

What is a habitat?

A **habitat** is a place in nature. Plants live in habitats. Animals live in habitats, too.

4

Living and non-living

There are **living things** in habitats. Plants and animals are living things. There are **non-living things** in habitats, too. Rocks, water, and ice are non-living things.

Everything they need

Plants and animals need air, water, and food to stay alive. Plants and animals find everything they need in their habitats. This leopard seal needs water in its habitat. It finds food in the water.

Food in the habitat

This bird is an albatross.
It finds everything it needs
in its habitat. The albatross
finds fish to eat in its habitat.

The Antarctic

The **Antarctic** is a habitat. The Antarctic is at the very bottom of Earth. It is very cold in the Antarctic. There is a lot of snow and ice in this habitat.

Antarctica

The land in the Antarctic is called **Antarctica**. Some parts of Antarctica are flat. Other parts have tall mountains. Antarctica is almost always covered with snow and ice.

The Southern Ocean

There is a very cold ocean in the
Antarctic. It is called the Southern
Ocean. Animals swim in this ocean.
Ice floats on parts of this ocean.
Some animals spend time on the ice.

Big bergs

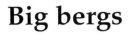

Huge chunks of ice float
in the Southern Ocean.
These chunks of ice
are called **icebergs**.

Antarctic weather

The weather in the Antarctic
is always cold. Freezing winds
blow almost every day. The
winds are strong. The wind is
blowing snow on these penguins.

Short summers

Antarctic summers are short. They
last for only a few weeks. Some
snow and ice melts in summer,
but the weather is still cold.

13

Antarctic plants

The Antarctic is too cold for most plants. Only a few plants grow there. Antarctic plants grow only in summer. They grow near **coasts**. Coasts are parts of land that are near oceans. This grass is growing near a coast.

Tiny plants

Millions of tiny plants grow in the Southern Ocean. They float near the top of the water. These ocean plants are called **phytoplankton**.

Phytoplankton can be seen only with a magnifying glass.

Plants make food

Living things need food to stay
alive. Plants make their own food.
They make food from sunlight,
air, and water. Making food
from sunlight, air, and water
is called **photosynthesis**.

Plant food

Phytoplankton make food from sunlight and water. Phytoplankton float near the top of the water where sunlight can reach them.

Sunlight shines on the top of the water.

Phytoplankton take in sunlight.

Phytoplankton use water to make food.

17

Antarctic animals

Look at the animals on these
pages. They live in the Antarctic.
Most Antarctic animals live in the
Southern Ocean. Some animals
leave the ocean and spend time
on the ice or on the rocks.

krill

albatross

Antarctic cod

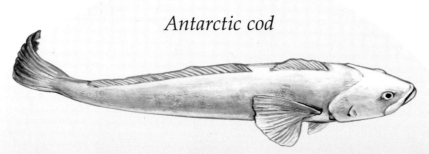

Antarctic
fur seal

king penguins

orca

Under the ice

There is a lot of ice on the Southern Ocean. The water under the ice is cold and dark. Some animals live in the water under the ice. The animals that you see here live under the ice in the Southern Ocean.

sea spider

squid

octopus

sea stars

clams

Out of the water

Penguins and seals live in water.
Sometimes they come out of the
water to rest on ice or on rocks.
They have babies on the ice or
on the rocks. These elephant
seals are resting on a big rock.

Having babies

Baby penguins are called chicks. This mother penguin is watching over her two chicks. The chicks are resting on some rocks.

Finding food

Animals must search to find food in the Antarctic. Some animals eat only plants. These animals are called **herbivores**. Krill are herbivores. They eat phytoplankton.

Meat-eaters

Some animals eat other animals. Animals that eat other animals are called **carnivores**. This orca is a carnivore. It eats fish, penguins, and seals.

Eating both

Other Antarctic animals are **omnivores**. Omnivores eat both plants and other animals. This Antarctic isopod is an omnivore. It eats dead plants and animals and anything else it can find!

Getting energy

sun

All living things need **energy**. They need energy to grow and to move. Energy comes from the sun. Plants get energy from the sun. Animals get energy by eating other living things. Krill are herbivores. They get energy by eating phytoplankton.

krill

phytoplankton

Eating krill

Many Antarctic animals
eat krill. This leopard
seal eats krill. It gets
energy from the krill.

Keeping warm

Antarctic animals must stay warm. Many animals have **blubber** under their skin. Blubber is thick layers of fat. Blubber helps keep animals warm. This blue whale has thick blubber under its skin.

Thick feathers

Antarctic birds have feathers.
Their feathers are very thick.
Feathers help keep birds warm.
This albatross has thick feathers.

Too cold

In winter, the Southern Ocean gets too cold for many Antarctic animals. Some animals must leave. They swim to warmer oceans in the winter. This fin whale is swimming to a warmer ocean.

Words to know and Index

animals
pages 4, 5, 6, 10, 18-19, 20, 24, 25, 26, 27, 28, 30

Antarctic
pages 8, 9, 10, 12, 13, 14, 18, 24, 25, 27, 28, 29, 30

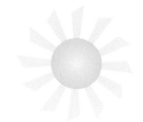

energy
pages 26, 27

food
pages 6, 7, 16, 17, 24

habitats
pages 4, 5, 6, 7, 8

ice
pages 5, 8, 9, 10, 11, 13, 18, 20, 22

plants
pages 4, 5, 6, 14-15, 16, 17, 24, 25, 26

swimming
pages 10, 30

Other index words

1 2 3 4 5 6 7 8 9 0   Printed in the U.S.A.   5 4 3 2 1 0 9 8 7 6